waiting
for
the wind

poems
by
jean lyford

Azalea Art Press
Berkeley . California

ISBN: 978-0-9899961-7-4

Other titles by Jean Lyford:

Waves of Time
Remembrances

Dedication:

For my family and many friends
who have shared this journey.

CONTENTS

November 2013

December 2013

January 2014

February 2014

March 2014

Foreword

As the leader of Hummingwords Writing Workshops, my life has been immeasurably enriched by writing with Jean every Wednesday for the past four years. Jean signed up for the very first Hummingwords session and has assumed her designated spot on the couch ever since as one of the most loyal and dedicated writers I've ever known. Her process of discovering her voice and exploring the themes that resonate with her has been a wonder to witness.

From the very beginning, Jean's writing has demonstrated that she is fearless when it comes to diving deep and exploring the dimly lit waters between the conscious and unconscious mind. She is equally at home in the abstract and emotional world of symbol, metaphor, and archetype as she is in the more concrete, rational realm of science.

Jean has implicit trust in the process of letting her muses speak through her without having to understand all the nuances of what they give her to say and why. Watching her create her poems, it seems as though her writing is guided from the deepest springs of her being.

Jean's poems, like those of Mary Oliver, interweave astute observations of the natural world with psychological insights and luminous mysteries shining beneath the surface. Her poems give us flights of ecstasy and plunges into grief, as well as a sense of bittersweet nostalgia regarding the process of looking back over memories to create a meaningful narrative of one's time on Earth.

When Jean was diagnosed with cancer last year, our very close community of writers was devastated right along with her. But in spite of having to decline all her other commitments so she could pursue treatment and conserve energy, Jean has remained a faithful writer, using the Amherst Writers and Artists Method to make sense of her emotions and experiences.

In her open and courageous investigation into the mysterious business of living and dying, Jean has taught us by example how to face one's mortality with clear eyes and an open heart. We are all deeply humbled by her example and honored to be a part of her beautiful life.

— Cynthia Leslie-Bole

Preface

The development of *Waiting for the Wind* arose out of several surprises. My first two books of poetry, *Waves of Time* and *Remembrances,* each were the result of two years of work. I did not expect to publish again after my last reading in June of 2013. However, life changed.

Last fall I was diagnosed with terminal 4th stage breast cancer that had spread to my bones. It explained why I had not been feeling well for almost a year, but nevertheless it came as a shock. Treatment that would be slowing the process, not curing it, began in September 2013. I absorbed the news and tried to come to terms with it by writing.

By November I found myself writing almost every day. There was something about centering my thoughts on what was happening to my body that helped me accept those changes. Poetry became a therapy, a comfort, a challenge—all that makes one human. I noticed tiny things around me. I wanted to let my essence appreciate these feelings, even the pain, because all experience became so real.

After realizing the need to continue to write poetry, I opened a new file called *Post-Cancer Poems.* The writing from November 2013 through March 2014 includes the poems written each month as I progressed through treatment and bodily changes. The response I received after sharing some of the poetry with others who also had cancer convinced me that a new book could be helpful to others going through the same process.

Here it is. May my poems provide solace and insight to those who read them.

— *Jean Lyford*
May 2014

If you reveal your secrets
to the wind, you should not blame
the wind for revealing them
to the trees.

– *Khalil Gibran*

waiting
for
the wind

November 2013

Embers

a familiar burn
blurring the dream
dying quietly
a white noise
finding focus
beyond pain
while embers
of memory
remain

Rest

quietude in the garden
savoring amber and wine
colors held gently
on leaf tips
waiting for rain
or wind
to help separate
the seasons
summer recedes
into a breathless
windless stasis
offering gifts
an enormous last rose
or bronze messengers
harbingers of fall
when frogs croak
by my window

An Eyelash of Time

an eyelash of time
a mere moment
an intrusive fleeting moment
when spirit sheds containment
wanders afar
wondering
dreaming
evolving into
an unfamiliar matrix
pretending to be real

Days Die Gently

days die gently
in the fading light
swallowed slowly
as sips of shadows
lengthen dusk
into a darkening night

Infinity

time stretches
across the years
offering possibilities
birthing ideas
suggesting action
holding the future
loosely
with room for change
elastic time
tires eventually
breaking infinite choices
into finite patterns
whirling us away

Leaves Hang Heavy

on branches bowed
by the weight of rain
fluttering
dropping
leaf by leaf
breaking away
falling slowly
wafting to and fro
finally
joining compatriots
in soggy clusters
under the Sycamore
forming a moist mass
nourishing the future

The Volunteer Sycamore

self seeding
leafed out
hand patterned
reversible
shining
then matte finished
turning toward one another
then fluttering away
ebbing
until
a sudden wind
undoes tranquility
the tree bends
leaves blow
inside out
until the next
wind tide surprises
as though
it never happened before

Now Is the Time

to care for things
put off before
so much time ahead
only a little left
do it while you can
leave instructions
tell all your secrets
at least most of them
study the garden
nestle into memory
visions of desert or bog
shade filtered light
New England saltboxes
gray clapboard
a touch of black
tones down brightness
sedate blues, greens
or yellows fading
yet standing firm
quiet guardians
of time

Barbs

barbs beneath
sting freely
without concern
living within
tasting, feeding
announcing
their presence

December 2013

Serpents in the Garden

hidden trails
tell of their meanderings
winding
threading new bobbins
sewing over our treasures
rediscovering
kindred souls

Lean Back

lean back carefully
slowly until the pillows' tufts
touch your back lightly
releasing stiffness
a sigh suffices
relieving pain for a moment
or announcing reality
borne on pointed wings
sharp edges
stinging a little
a brief electric shock
passing quickly
just a reminder
from a stoic tutor
bearing pain
flying
floating it away

Bones or Beams

home to creatures
of the night
stirring
creeping
burrowing
feeding
weakening
house beams
or body bones
sapping strength
from whatever
bears weight
until night creatures
have their fill
riding the fall
joining the rubble
of demolished
cannibalized
bones or beams

Winter Leaves

winter leaves
underfoot now
bare branches extend
protecting fragile limbs
Japanese maples
are coy in their gentility
the Sycamore resists ceding power
as its arms turn sienna
in the rain
deeper in understanding
willing to watch
the seasons change
even though days darken
and nights chill

Deep Down

deep down
slivers sleep
waiting for sparks
to illuminate their presence
to explode in tiny fires
to announce recognition
of their being
of their fury
as they climb
out of the deep
into my being

Anger

what is anger for?
mojo?
adrenaline energy?
a sense of self?
an ability to defend?
a source for retribution?
I do not know but
it doesn't feel good
nor truly justified
nor admirable
nor signify a life
a core of self
able
strong
in control
but rather
a fault
a reminder
of one's
humanity

Let the Future Be

whatever it will be
no longer seeking fun
nor even companionship
no longer doing the should
nor wondering about the would
nor even the maybe
just doing what one can
whenever able or pushed
into something
anything
beyond coping
within realistic bounds
embracing the possible
sustaining the present
letting the future
worry about itself

Heavy Air

holding
clinging to itself
bits of earth
floats of
sandy streams
arrested by time
lingering
watching
waiting
for the wind

Stillness

soundlessly
stillness
surrounds me
taking me
to another place
where thoughts
wander
in and out
of consciousness
encircle
awareness
gird it into
a postcard memory
a New York City
back yard
snowed in peace
covered in purity
holding me safe

Cards

happy faces
smile at me
messages from
others' lives
another year
exciting travels
proud successes
no obits here
nor complaints
nor burdens to share
nothing awry
only joy
filling time
with worthy pursuits
tell me how it feels
not how it looks
so I will know
the card is real

Light

light's wandering path
born beyond the unseen crest
traverses the hillside
trembles on high
before sweeping into
its Z formation
then hesitating
creeping along
until gaining speed
illuminating motion
cradling curves
slowly at bends
before the inevitable
flow falls into
a gleaming puddle of light

January 2014

Is There a Place?

is there a place—
safe, quiet
a limbo light
glowing
refreshing hope
recharging dreams
soothing pain?
is there such a place—
carousing in my mind
diving into wells
entangling awareness
enfolding thoughts
remolding them
into clumps of cares
ready for recycling
while cleaning house
forgetting time
waiting patiently
for what may come?

Not Knowing

a painful state
when time stops
becomes trackless
unsustainable
lost to action
left to wondering
hoping
fearing
writing stories
without an end

Brittle

brittle as my bones
dry grass crackling
under foot
bare trees on brown hills
begging for relief
even frost
to seal the earth
with sparkles
dew-like
in the wrong season
pretending to be rain

Lunch with Friends

a day together
full of smiles
sharing funny stories
a tear or two
between laughs
whatever separates
conjoins
delves into the place
where friendship abides

Dreaming

awake or asleep
defying emptiness
engendering hope
images
fantasies
realities
mix together
in a brew
a teapot of possibilities
blending the past
adjusting the present
parsing pain until
visions melt away

Silhouettes

black arms
leafless
dry silhouettes
against a pale sky
on a still day
stretch out
yearning
awaiting the wind
when branch touches branch
whispering
planning ahead
comforting one another
while dreaming of spring

The Lazy Sun

the lazy sun
peeks through the trees
pale, diluted
in its winter light
weakened yet still faithful
arising each day
staying a little longer
until strong enough
to share its warmth

Suns at Night

suns wink at night
enticing us to join
their club
the only initiation fee
imagining
the improbable
or the impossible
a sense of other creatures
somewhere
somehow
unlike us
better or worse
but blinking
calling us
to another galaxy
or perhaps just next door

Winter Trees

pruned
bare black limbs
undressed
stretch out
shivering in the wind
hardening
while waiting
for cover
guarding
incipient green's
promise of spring

A Warm Day

confuses azaleas
a few blooms
light up by day
then shrivel
drop blossoms
on cold nights
another warm day
invites new blooms
pretending warmth will last
that light will spread
lingering
through winter's pain
long enough to survive

A New Lump

a sac of creatures
waiting their turn
released from bonds
wandering freely
finding distant homes
flourishing
invisible
unknown nibblers
feeding
gnawing on my bones

A Reprieve

but no joy
too deep into
dying?
too weary to
believe?
too suspicious of
hope?
false courage
covering fear and pain?
wanting
peace
sleep
a defined time
to end the waiting?

An Old Pine

bends in the wind
branches curl
into swirls of twigs
ready to break
awaiting a fall
when large branches
crack and split
showing their essence
drying sap
resin of life
mixing with needles
softening their sharpness
leaving behind
a life lived
in the aroma of pine

A Rose in Winter

I want to be a rose in winter
dropping blood red petals in the snow
lasting beyond the season
both a memory
and a promise
to bloom again

Curves

a vole's rounded back
a deer path on the hillside
arced around a pine
pruned bushes
groomed round
contrasting
stalks of drying weeds

notice all the curves
places where shadows
fade into the background
accepting interference
adding balance
quietly
unobtrusively
guarding
touching
embracing
human need

Awakening Trees

white or pink dots
adorn plum trees'
bare branches
new life
puffs of blooms
filling spaces
delineating
tree shapes to come
after blossom confetti
blows away
revealing
bursts of green

Bed

I want to stay in bed
bend my knees
wiggle the soles of my feet
until they warm
on the fleece fiber sheet
nestle my hips
into foam memory
snuggle my back
until pain disappears
melting into softness
a cat wrapped in its own fur
content in senseful safety
one eye open
waiting
just in case
I have to leave this bed

Caress the Soil

sitting in my garden
caressing the soil
a palmful falls between my fingers
damp, living soil
humus fresh
ready for planting

I gather soil
scooping it up
piling into mounds
Kentucky Wonder bean seeds
sit ready
waiting for fingers
to poke them into a deep mound
where roots can grow
rain runs off
until the first two leaves
open to the air

damp soil collects on my pants
but no matter
I scoot along
form new mounds
squeeze the soil
hold it to my face
fertile soil
sweet in its fecundity
three seeds per mound

after two completed rows
I stretch out on the ground
slightly chilled
lost in the present
a weak sun on my face
earthworms
curling around my fingers

I smile
my home the garden
a place where doubts
are buried
where life continues
enfolding me
as I caress the earth

Who Watches?

behind the tree
that one
the elder over there
someone watches
someone or something watches me
eyes bright
reflecting sun or moon
day or night
never alone
a being, an entity watches
bodiless in the dark
veiled gauze by day
only eyes
amber or turquoise
colored by mood

its or mine?
unblinking eyes
drill through me
pierce me
open me
release me
a magnetic force

what creature is this?
whose eyes are these?
an animal?

a silent owl by night
catching moonbeams
a skittish fawn by day
with luminous eyes
or
could it be a mirror
capturing my being
piercing my depths
into what lies hidden
trying to be recognized?

February 2014

Sun's Day

the sun carries mist
on its back
a veiled light
diffusing fog
rolling in from the sea
illuminating the hills
into softness
floating water colors
brushing the landscape
dissolving fog
in the noon sun
fusing its rays
until
reappearing
as orange and pink
fingers cascading
a roiling mist
over the hills
and the fading sun sets
swallowed by dusk
surrendering
into sleep
and darkness

Stepping Stones

delineate a path
curving
inviting
creatures to follow
a safe way
a trail of aromas
through a garden
or across a stream
to discovery
new thoughts
new beauty
finding peace

Actors Unseen

raccoons were here
last night
I can tell
they never replace drain covers
their reservoirs for washing worms
the lawn scraped
searching for food

raccoons leave large swaths
even in the dying grass
skunks scrape more delicately
without leaving a scent
moles and gophers stay undercover
designing lacework tunnels
eating roots or burrowed grubs
opossums skitter about in shadows
avoiding marauders

coyotes join at pre-dawn
stalking rodents or
cats let out too early
by day they disappear
hide from us
letting us pretend
we command
our well-tended gardens

the scratched earth
the abandoned cover
left as casual messages
of thanks

Garden Birds

the steller's jay
named for its beauty
still squawks
in my garden
sits on a pine branch
surveying
stealing eggs
guarding
bullying
any other bird
especially small finches or wrens
unable to hold their own
in a fight
but their songs
so lyrical
so lilting
gentle to the ear
capture the day

Rain at Last

as drops fall
lift your face
feel the coolness
pings of droplets
hesitating
sliding down your cheeks
forming a rivulet
escaping
wandering
dripping
off your chin
finding home
down your neck
warming
tickling
sharing
the joy of rain

The Hills Are Green

again
rain has softened
dry weeds
bent them
puffed them up
and turned them green
alive
blending colors
into shadows
or curved paths
delineating
repainting
bold patterns
signs of new life
bursting forth
on the hills

Be Mindful

if I judge myself harshly
I practice judging others

if I accept change readily
I find positive purpose

if I complain frequently
I engender pity in others
as well as myself

if I laugh heartedly
I share joy

if I let tears flow unabashedly
I share empathy

if I notice my surroundings deeply
I become one with nature

if I offer love to others and myself
I spread caring thoughts

if I respect others for themselves
I respect myself

if I embrace curiosity
I stay young in spirit

if I give openly to others
I fulfill my needs as well

these are my precepts
this is what I honor
this is how I want to live

Bursts of White

the rounded viburnum
shows off clusters
of tiny blossoms
gathered on the ends
of trimmed branches
bursting forth
a white explosion
competing
with plum trees
background or
companions
to white narcissus
ivory and gold
reflecting light
heralding
a new season
when pastel tulips
add depth
to daffodils

Pots Wait

for new growth
another chance
to flourish
to hold tall fronds
silvery green
with a touch of
geranium rose
braiding into
trailing blue
petunias
the pots wait
dreaming
of how they'll look
remembering
last year's blooms
wanting
rebirth
in new soil
with fresh makeup
ready for
a starring role

Last Gasp

is the last gasp
somehow the best?
gentle flutters
with skips
leaving spaces
for unused beats
then restarts
unfriendly in the dark
though comforting
by day
a lady-like snort
as if even sleep
could not be crude
mesmerizing puffs
a background for smiles
wandering thoughts
reviewing a life
still warm in memory
still beckoning
still breezing
white noise
misty voices
whispering off and on
sharing shadows
clearing cobwebs
touching waves
of truth

as breaths pitch high
then stop just before
the rooster crows

Clouds

float above
shading the sun
protecting the sky
softening
the scene
binding blueness
swirling in islands
leaping shapes
of imaginary scenes

Wandering Light

light wanders
through the trees
dissolving patterns
dancing
melting away
then coming together
in a new design
a jolly form
full of energy
a rousing rhythm
bending
stepping high
a cheerful jitterbug
until the waltz begins

Rain Returns

clearing the air
cleansing leaves
bending daffodils
dampening earth
releasing scents
of fecundity
gentle gasps
test air cleansed
of dust and mites
rain drops
run into rivulets
carrying pollen
to a new place
back to earth
where life begins

March 2014

Silent Birds

flutter to the feeder
yellow finches
mouths full of seeds
tails maneuvering
as they sway
keeping beaks
aligned
feet curled
clutching a perch
claiming their turn to feed
while tiny black-capped chickadees
flapping impatient wings
hover
squawklessly
silently awaiting
a table at the feast

where are the songs
backyard birds
used to sing?
those songs
I almost remember
at least the lilt
the joy of voicing
contentment
or warnings
in a minor key?

perhaps they still sing
but not with full mouths
or perhaps
even though they sing
I no longer hear them

Mother Tongue

the body speaks
whether or not
we choose to listen
soft gentle sounds
cuddled in contentment
in the flush
of sustenance

when heard
it is the body
of a healthy animal
dozing in the sun
dreamless
wrapped in wistfulness
without words

if unheard
the body's voice
becomes insistent
full of words
a language more harsh
a tongue more twisted
a different creature
centered on self
unable to exude
in peace

insistence grows
anger rises
from
denying needs and messages
the body becomes
an alien chariot
caught
in a civil war

remember
to stretch in the sun
to snuggle away
pain or fear
to speak your
Mother Tongue

Disappearing Days

where do days go
after I am through with them?
after time devours them
or hides them
in corners of my mind
inaccessible
slow moving neurons
clog memory
glom pathways
into a tangle of time
short-circuited
frayed
but still extant
to reappear
only in dreams

Turning

turning toward the sun
creeping
in unseen motion
ignored
waiting
alone on the sill
begging for water
as well as sun
somehow staying alive
the cactus leans
away from shade
touching the window
swelling
saving fluid
while stretching
reaching
for the sun
until
the pot is turned

Mindful Body

flights of fancy
buoy the mind
let it float
on a sea of choice
whether rough or still
rolling or resting
until
aches interfere

fantasy dissolves
becoming
a watchful guardian
transporting recognition
honoring body's needs
packing them up
in a secret purse
saving awareness for
a more convenient time
when memory
opens the purse
lets pain pour out
finds words
for
future fantasies

Memories

are me
born in the now
a place of being
of choices
where memories are formed
or denied entry
into the storage bank
fondled
kneaded
shaped
improved upon
colored into
ingredients for dreams

new memories
spring forth
melding axons
into loves or losses
saving bits for future savor
opening secret drawers
or quickly slamming them shut

I become
manager of truth
creator of hope
denier of fears
if memory disappears
so will my essence

Trees

sun umbrellas
cozy-up the garden
giving depth to vision
shade shapes canopies
bronze or lime green
defines edges
catching light on leaf tips

fruit trees take turns
adding blossoms
mauve or white
hovering over primrose eyes
that ogle bees

low branches provide
nesting places
new life
fills spaces
waiting to be mixed
into a new alchemy

Change

is not sudden
it creeps unobserved
waiting for notice
acceptance
appreciation
new possibilities
while
carrying seasons
on its back
easing into or out of life
greening or drying
secreted into memory
where change becomes awareness

I've been here before

Dandelions

flourish in adversity
seeds drop
into a pocket of dirt
germinate
bounce into color
rough leaves
cling to earth
refuse to abandon
their golden centers
patient
claiming
their right
to belong
to share dew
with the noblest
to spread their seeds
wherever the wind will carry them

Shelf Life

my shelf life
has gathered dust
I sneeze just thinking of it
and then I laugh
this will not pass so soon

my shelf sits
waiting
empty jars
lids nearby
wait to be filled
glass stoppers
oval or rounded
roll about

once favorites
are now kept as souvenirs
of times that were
of bangled wrists
and stockinged feet
of disjointed fingers
crooked
in a gesture
almost obscene
but not quite

glass scratching on glass
bone squeaking on bone

will come soon enough
or not soon enough
to calm a wobbly self
uncomfortable
in an old skin
too weak
to form a new one

a fleeting thought
in a darkened room
echoes with long gone voices
fluttering about
ignoring me

I want to talk to them
but strands of understanding
stay slack
do not wave vibrating sounds
of caring

I listen
to the voice of silence
that will not let me in
holding me alone in company
a voyager passing through
noticing the stars
but unable to touch them

Crumbs

a pile of crumbs
not just a few
dropped
from a child's cookie
grainy
not sweet

the crumbs of living
what termites
and carpenter ants
eat
while weakening wood
to make a nest

crumbs of leftovers
when what is wanted dies
the tombstone's resting place
for what might have been
but wasn't
still leaving a trace

personal crumbs
telling tales of long journeys
treks through adversity
micro-survivals

crumbs carrying wind
in their grains
sharing memories
whispering in alien ears
spreading the news
tickling bare skin

crumbs of rock and wood
slivers of ancient arms
lacerating time
if felt too quickly
sharing minuscule exploding
atoms of awareness

Becalmed

waiting for the wind
to carry me
out to sea
sails set for adventure
hair blowing across my face
shaking hands
holding
resisting
the wind's pull
until its insistence
overpowers
my feeble efforts
carries me
wandering willy-nilly
leaving purpose behind
floating
on the tips of waves
until the ebb and flow
floats me back to shore

Acknowledgments

I have received such abundant support from family and friends through these past six months that it would take another book to name everyone. But those who drove me to appointments and treatments, brought meals, made visits, shopped for me or sent cards and words of encouragement know who you are. I bless you all. Members of the Orinda Woman's Club, the Rotary Club of Orinda, Hummingwords, the 3-5'ers—I hope you know that I can never describe how much I appreciate your help.

Special thanks go to Cynthia Leslie-Bole for prodding me to think of another book and then taking on the editing job. Karen Mireau, the publisher, organized *Waiting for the Wind,* and helped with decision making when it was hard for me to think beyond nausea. Both Cynthia's and Karen's patience kept me going.

About the Author

Jean Lyford was born and raised in suburban Philadelphia. After graduating college, she moved to New York City with her first husband, Gerald McKee.

While living in New York she met and married her second husband Joseph Lyford, with whom she had two children, Amy and Joseph, Jr.

The family moved to California in 1966 when her husband became Professor of Journalism at U.C. Berkeley. They settled in Orinda, California, where Jean pursued her own career as an educator.

Jean still lives in the same house where she raised her children, surrounded by her grandchildren Eve and Willa, and the garden that has been her constant source of poetic inspiration.

Contact:

Jean Lyford
Author
mjlyford@comcast.net

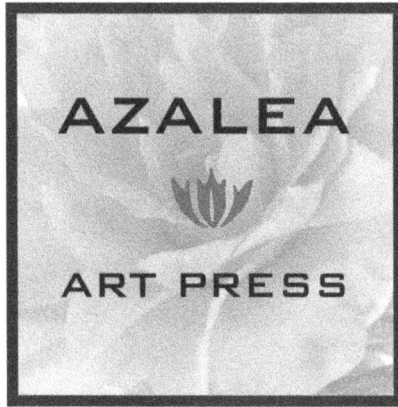

Karen Mireau
Publisher
Azalea Art Press
azaleaartpress@gmail.com

Book Orders
www.lulu.com